CONTENTS

T0005040

Did you know?

Discover some interesting facts about Greek myths.

WHO'S WHO?

Find out more about some of the main characters in Greek myths.

MYTH LINKS

Learn about similar characters or stories from other cultures.

ANCIENT GREECE

Today, Greece is a European country made up of the mainland and over 2,000 islands. In ancient Greece, the area wasn't a country but a collection of individual settlements that gradually grew into city-states. Some of these were outside the area we know as Greece today. Each community had a very strong sense of identity.

This satellite photo shows the areas of ancient Greece. Greek civilization covered a wide area, including parts of modern-day Turkey.

GREEK
MYTHS AND
LEGENDS

Jilly Hunt

Chicago, Illinois

© 2014 Raintree
an imprint of Capstone Global Library, LLC
Chicago, Illinois

To contact Capstone Global Library, please
call 800-747-4992, or visit our web site,
www.capstonepub.com

Edited by Nancy Dickmann and Abby Colich
Designed by Jo Hinton-Malivoire
Original illustrations © Capstone Global Library
   Ltd 2013
Illustrations by Xöul
Picture research by Elizabeth Alexander
Production by Victoria Fitzgerald
Originated by Capstone Global Library Ltd

**Library of Congress Cataloging-in-
Publication Data**
Hunt, Jilly.
   Greek myths and legends / Jilly Hunt.—1
[edition].
     p. cm.—(All about myths)
   Includes bibliographical references and index.
   ISBN 978-1-4109-5468-8 (hb)—ISBN 978-1-4109-
5474-9 (pb) — ISBN 978-1-4109-6598-1 (ss) 1.
Mythology, Greek—Juvenile literature. I. Title.

   BL783.H865 2013
   398.20938—dc23   2012043972

Acknowledgments
We would like to thank the following for
permission to reproduce photographs:
Alamy: ACE STOCK LIMITED, 18, Ancient Art
and Architecture, 6, bilwissedition Ltd. & Co.
KG, 31, Chronicle, 28, INTERFOTO, 15, 19,
Juniors Bildarchiv GmbH, 23, The Art Archive,
35; Art Resource, NY: BnF, Dist. RMN-Grand
Palais, 36; Bridgeman Images: Adam, Lambert-
Sigisbert (1700-59)/Louvre, Paris, France, 13,
Museum of Fine Arts, Boston, Massachusetts,
USA, Museum purchase with funds donated
in honor of Edward W. Forbes, 7, Tiepolo,
Giovanni Battista (Giambattista) (1696-1770)/
Palazzo Sandi-Porto (Cipollato), Venice, Italy,
24; Capstone: Xoul, 11, 21, 27, 33, 39, 41; Getty
Images: Fine Art Photographic, 34, Robbie Jack,
40; Shutterstock: Anastasios71, Design Element,
arogant, Design Element, arosoft, Design Element,
Cyril Hou, 14, Fat Jackey, Design Element,
Georgy Markov, 29, javarman, Design Element,
luigi nifosi, Design Element, Pshenichka, Design
Element, Ralf Siemieniec, 25, S.Borisov, 16, Scott
Norsworthy, Design Element, Timur Kulgarin,
22, V J Matthew, 5, Vangelis76, Design Element;
Shutterstock Premier: Cci, 17; SuperStock: Anatoly
Sapronenkov, 30, Fine Art Photographic Library,
37, Silvio Fiore, Cover, 9, Universal Images, 4,
Wolfgang Kaehler, 12, World History Archive, 8

The publishers would like to thank Robert Parker
for his invaluable assistance in the production of
this book.

In ancient Greece, plays were performed in honor of the gods. We can still see some of their large, open-air theaters today.

SHARED BELIEFS

Ideas spread between these communities, and they often shared language, beliefs, and stories. Myths and legends were handed down from generation to generation, but they were not always written down, so many details changed over time. New beliefs were adopted or combined with others as the Greeks came into contact with other cultures.

WHO'S WHO?

Hesiod, who probably lived around 700 BCE, was one of the earliest Greek poets. He wrote epics such as *Theogony* and *Works and Days*. *Theogony* explains the origin of the world and the family tree of the gods. *Works and Days* gives moral and practical advice by using myths as examples.

Did you know?

The word "myth" comes from the Greek word *mythos*, meaning "story," "word," "saying," or "fiction."

ORIGIN STORIES

Today, scientists can explain how the world began using scientific findings, but in the past people used mythology to make sense of it. Many cultures have myths connected with the origin of the world.

OUT OF CHAOS

The ancient Greeks believed that at first there was Chaos, and that this was a dark nothingness. Out of Chaos came a creator force called Gaia, or Mother Earth. They believed that Gaia then gave birth to the different parts of the universe, including Uranus, who was the sky, Ourea, the mountains, and Pontus, the sea.

THE EARLIEST CREATURES ON EARTH

Gaia and Uranus had children, who were the earliest creatures to live on Earth. Among the first creatures were the giants called Cyclopes. These giants looked like people but only had one eye. Uranus worried that the Cyclopes were going to steal his power, so he was cruel to them and banished them to the Underworld.

Next, Gaia and Uranus produced some powerful children called the Titans. These incredibly strong giants grew up to rule over Earth. The Titans began to have children of their own, and some of these children would become the most powerful gods and goddesses of ancient Greek beliefs. They were known as the Olympians.

Gaia was not happy about the way Uranus treated her offspring, the Cyclopes.

Did you know?

In the Greek language Cyclops means "Round Eye." In some myths, Cyclopes were said to be cannibals.

MYTH LINKS

The Keres people are American Indians from the southwest, and they also have a myth about the creation of the universe. They believe that the Thinking Woman created the world by weaving her own thoughts.

CLASH OF THE TITANS

Gaia wanted the Titans to seek revenge on Uranus. She encouraged Cronus to lead the Titans in a rebellion. They defeated Uranus, and Cronus became king.

But Cronus had been warned that one of his children would kill him. When his wife, Queen Rhea, had children, Cronus swallowed them up so that they couldn't kill him. Finally, Rhea fooled her husband by giving him a stone wrapped in swaddling clothes instead of the baby named Zeus. Cronus swallowed the stone, and Zeus was smuggled away to live in Crete.

Cronus was the youngest of the 12 Titans from Gaia and Uranus.

THE REVENGE OF ZEUS

Zeus heard about what his father had done and was determined to seek revenge. He returned to Greece and sneaked a magical drug into Cronus's drink. Cronus vomited up the five children that he had swallowed: Poseidon, Hades, Hestia, Demeter, and Hera.

Zeus battled against King Cronus and the other Titans. He freed the Cyclopes and, in return, they provided powerful weapons—thunderbolts for Zeus, a forked trident for Poseidon, and an invisibility helmet for Hades. Eventually the Titans were defeated, and Zeus became the king of all the gods.

■ Zeus was seen as an all-powerful god who would hurl thunderbolts when angry.

The Final Battle

After their victory against the Titans, the three brothers relaxed in the sunshine at the top of Mount Olympus as they discussed what was to happen with the universe.

"Let's draw lots," suggested Poseidon. Zeus gathered up three sticks to use—one representing the Heavens, one for the Oceans, and one for the Underworld.

"I'll draw first," he said, as he pulled out the Heavens stick.

"Your turn next," he said, as he stretched out toward Poseidon.

"Ah, the Oceans. That means the Underworld for you, Hades." Hades nodded.

"The big problem is what to do with the Titans. We don't want them coming back," Zeus said, as he began to pace.

"Seems to me the only answer is Tartarus. We'll throw them in and set giants to guard the gates. They'll never escape." Hades nodded again in agreement.

When Gaia, the mother of the Titans, heard the news she was furious!

"I'll make the Olympians pay!" she bellowed.

"I'll give him one more battle." Gaia made her way to see her youngest son, Typhon. Typhon was a monster with a hundred serpent heads, and Gaia was confident that he would defeat the powerful Zeus.

Gaia watched as Zeus hurled thunderbolt after thunderbolt at Typhon's heads. The battle was not going well. Typhon was cornered on the island of Sicily. Zeus picked up the fiery volcano, Mount Etna, and hurled it at the monster. The battle was over, and Gaia could do no more. Zeus was now the supreme ruler of the universe.

GODS AND GODDESSES

The ancient Greeks believed in a big group of gods and goddesses. They were known as the Olympians because they lived on Mount Olympus. Each god was thought to have power over a particular area of the world or life. If the Greeks needed something, they would ask the relevant god. For example, for a good harvest they would ask Demeter, goddess of the earth, farming, and harvest, for help.

Hera was the daughter of King Cronos and Queen Rhea. She became queen of the gods.

Did you know?

The ancient Greeks believed that gods looked like humans, and that they got married, had children, and argued. But unlike mortal humans, gods were immortal, meaning they lived forever.

THE POWERFUL ONES

Zeus was the leader of the Olympians and was also god of the skies. Hera was the queen of the gods and ruled over marriage. She was Zeus's wife as well as his sister, and her jealousy over Zeus's behavior often caused trouble. Poseidon, one of Zeus's brothers, was god of the sea. This was an important god to a seafaring nation. He had an angry temper and could stir up great storms at sea with the trident given to him by the Cyclopes. Hades was god of the dead and ruled the Underworld. Demeter and Hestia were Zeus's other two sisters. Hestia was goddess of the hearth and ruled over domestic life. Demeter was goddess of farming and the harvest.

Poseidon, called Neptune in Rome, is shown holding a trident, conquering the waves.

MYTH LINKS

The Romans had gods of their own, with their own names. But some of the names have similar roots in Latin. When the Romans came into contact with the Greeks, they thought that the Greek gods sounded similar. They decided that Zeus was the same as their Jupiter, Hera the same as their Juno, and so on.

CHILDREN OF THE OLYMPIAN GODS

Zeus and Hera were the parents of Ares (the god of war), Hephaestus (the god of fire and volcanoes), and Hebe (the goddess of youth). Zeus also gave birth to a fully-grown Athena from his head. Athena was Zeus's favorite child. She was the goddess of war, wisdom, and arts and crafts.

Sometimes gods and goddesses had offspring with other people. If the other parent was immortal, for example a Titan, then the offspring would also be immortal. For example, Apollo and Artemis were the children of Zeus and a Titan named Leto. Apollo became the god of the sun and the arts, and Artemis was the goddess of hunting and childbirth. Zeus had a son with Maia, daughter of the Titan Atlas. Their child was Hermes (messenger of gods). His role included leading the dead down to Hades.

If a god had a child with a mortal, for example a human, then the child would have special powers but would be mortal, meaning they would die. They were often called heroes or demigods. Greek heroes would go on amazing adventures and have to fight terrifying mythical creatures (see pages 22–33).

This is a statue of Artemis, one of the children of Zeus and Leto.

WHO'S WHO: THE GREEK GODS AND GODDESSES

GREEK NAME	AREA OF POWER	ROMAN NAME
Aphrodite	love and beauty	Venus
Apollo	the sun and the arts	Apollo
Ares	war	Mars
Artemis	hunting and childbirth	Diana
Athena	war, wisdom, and crafts	Minerva
Demeter	farming and the harvest	Ceres
Dionysus	wine	Bacchus
Hades	the dead and the Underworld	Pluto
Hephaestus	fire and volcanoes	Vulcan
Hera	queen of the gods and ruler of marriage	Juno
Hermes	messenger of the gods	Mercury
Hestia	the hearth and domestic life	Vesta
Poseidon	the sea	Neptune
Zeus	supreme leader and god of the skies	Jupiter

This is an illustration of Hermes, messenger of the gods.

WORSHIPING THE GODS

Worshiping the gods was an important part of life in ancient Greece. Often, a family would pray at the altar in their home. Throughout the day, people would say prayers to particular gods as they performed their daily activities.

TEMPLES

The ancient Greeks built beautiful buildings called temples for the gods to live in. People would come to the temples to offer sacrifices. At the temple of Poseidon, people would make offerings and sacrifices to protect them from storms when they were going on a sea journey.

COMMUNICATING WITH THE GODS

The ancient Greeks believed that the gods would send messages, called oracles, to people through priests or priestesses. The place where the priest or priestess delivered the oracles is also known as an oracle. The Temple of Apollo at Delphi was the site of the most important oracle, known as the Delphic oracle. A story says that Zeus released two eagles from each end of the world, and where they met in the middle, a special temple to Apollo was built.

This is the Parthenon in Athens, the temple built to honor Athena. We can still see the building today.

Scientists have discovered ethylene gas escaping from rocks at Delphi. This gas could have made the priestess hallucinate and believe she could speak to the gods.

MYTH -LiNKS

The Vikings believed that prophetesses called volvas could communicate with the gods. Other cultures had different ways of communicating with the gods. For example, Siberian shaman and Native American medicine men would enter into a trance by drumming, dancing, and chanting in order to communicate with the spirit world.

■ This ancient Greek pot shows athletes in a running event.

FESTIVALS AND GAMES

The ancient Greeks held festivals to honor their gods. The Greeks thought these events would please the gods and make them more likely to grant their wishes. The festivals involved offerings and prayers but might also include athletic games, music, poetry recitals, or plays—these were seen as gifts to the gods. The Olympic Games were the most important games and were part of the festival held in honor of Zeus at a place called Olympia. The plays performed at such festivals tell us a lot about Greek myths.

Did you know?

If an ancient Greek wanted to know what the future held for him, he would consult a soothsayer or get the omens read. The omens were read by soothsayers who predicted the future by looking at the way a bird flew, or even by examining the internal organs of sacrificed animals!

OFFENDING THE GODS

The ancient Greeks really did not want to offend the gods. Different gods liked different sacrifices, which varied from cakes, to wine, to birds or animals. The sacrifices might be rejected if the rules weren't followed. Offending the gods could have serious consequences! For example, Athena (goddess of cloth-makers and embroiderers) turned a young woman named Arachne into a spider for boasting about how good she was at weaving.

■ It is from the name Arachne that we get the scientific name for spiders.

Tantalizing Tantalus

Zeus was fuming—the latest feast on Mount Olympus had not gone well. A mortal, Tantalus, had been the guest, but not only had he stolen the gods' special food to give it away to the mortals, he had also tried to trick the gods by cooking and serving his own son!

"Find him. He must be punished!" Zeus raged. "Who does he think he is? Trying to feed us human flesh! What kind of fool does he take me for?"

In his fury, Zeus hurled thunderbolts while he thought about how to punish Tantalus. Then he smiled craftily. He'd had an idea.

Tantalus soon found himself in the depths of Tartarus. He was standing in a pool of cool water up to his neck, but overhanging the pool was some delicious-looking fruit. "This doesn't seem too bad," he thought to himself. "I expected much, much worse. You're getting slack, Zeus."

It was another hot and sunny day, and Tantalus was grateful that he was in the shade of a tree with water to drink and fruit to eat. He stretched up to reach a piece of fruit, but the wind blew the branch just out of reach.

"Never mind," thought Tantalus, "I'll have a drink first." He bent forward to sip some of the water he was standing in, but as he did so, the water level lowered. He couldn't bend down far enough—the water kept moving.

"Strange," he thought, "but I'll try the fruit again. The wind seems to be calmer now." However, a gust of wind blew the fruit out of reach again, and then he noticed something. A great big boulder was hidden by the branches of the tree. It was straight above him.

"If those branches give way I'll be crushed! I understand now," he wept. "I'm to be forever tormented—thirsty, hungry, and always in fear of pain."

If you have ever been "tantalized," then you'll know how Tantalus felt!

HEROES AND BEASTS

The ancient Greeks believed that Earth had many strange and dangerous creatures living there. Some mythical beasts looked like ordinary animals but had a special power. For example, Pegasus looked like a normal horse but had wings and could fly. Monsters were often creatures made up of more than one animal—the Chimera was part lion, middle part goat, and back part serpent. These mythical creatures provided a perfect opportunity for a hero to show his strength and bravery.

Perseus was careful never to look directly at Medusa, so that he wouldn't be turned to stone.

PERSEUS AND MEDUSA

The legendary Greek hero Perseus was the son of Zeus and Princess Danae. He took on a dangerous challenge in order to protect his mother. King Polydectes wanted to marry Princess Danae, but she didn't want to marry him. Polydectes wanted Perseus out of the way, so he sent Perseus to kill Medusa the Gorgon—a hideous monster with snakes for hair who turned people to stone if they looked at her.

Perseus was helped in his quest by the goddess Athena, who gave him a reflective shield so that he would never have to look directly at Medusa. Perseus chopped off Medusa's head while she was asleep and took it back with him in a bag. He rescued his mother and turned Polydectes to stone with Medusa's head.

MYTH LINKS

Perhaps the ancient Greeks told stories about monsters in an attempt to explain natural events. For example, the Greeks told stories of the monster Typhon being buried under Mount Etna. This was a way of explaining the flames that came from the mountain.

Did you know?

It is said that Perseus returned home riding Pegasus, the winged horse that sprang from Medusa's blood.

After killing the Chimera, Bellerophon and Pegasus went on to have many more adventures together.

BELLEROPHON AND THE CHIMERA

The winged horse Pegasus also appears in other Greek myths. In the story of Bellerophon and the Chimera, Pegasus helps the hero to defeat a terrifying monster. Bellerophon was sent to kill the Chimera by the king of Lycia. Athena helped him by letting him use Pegasus. Nobody could get near the fire-breathing beast but, on the back of Pegasus, Bellerophon was able to fire arrows down on him from above.

AN UNHAPPY ENDING

Ancient Greek myths often taught people how to behave, and this story of Bellerophon doesn't have a happy ending for the hero. He became too proud of his achievements and tried to fly to the home of the gods, Olympus. Zeus was outraged that he had come uninvited, and decided Bellerophon had to be punished. Zeus caused Pegasus to throw off his rider, and Bellerophon fell to his death.

MYTH LINKS

Fire-breathing creatures, especially dragons, are common in many European myths. European dragons are usually fearsome, but Chinese dragons are kindly and wise.

THE MINOTAUR

One of the most famous monsters in Greek mythology is the Minotaur. This half-man, half-bull was kept in a specially designed Labyrinth by King Minos of Crete, near his palace at Knossos. Minos demanded that every 9 years the people of Athens send 14 young men and women for the Minotaur to eat.

MYTH LINKS

In 1900, the archaeologist Sir Arthur Evans discovered the ruins of a luxury palace at Knossos that he named the Palace of Minos. The palace would have contained many rooms, perhaps giving rise to the idea of the Labyrinth.

Theseus and the Minotaur

Aegeus, King of Athens, was distraught.

"Don't go, son!" he begged. "You'll never be able to slay the Minotaur."

But Theseus was determined as he boarded the ship with the other young men and women being sent to Crete. A black sail on their ship was a sign of mourning for the human sacrifices. Theseus's father embraced him.

"When the ship returns, you must raise the white sails so I know you're alive," said Aegeus.

Ariadne, the daughter of King Minos, was watching as the ship arrived. She saw Theseus and immediately fell in love with him. She promised to help him if he would marry her, and he agreed.

That night she sneaked past the guards and gave Theseus a sword and a magic ball of twine.

"Tie one end to the entrance and let it unwind as you work your way through the maze," she whispered. "You can follow it to find your way out again, after you kill the Minotaur."

The next morning, Theseus tied the magic twine to the entrance and bravely made his way into the maze, unwinding the twine as he went. As he got closer to the center, he could hear the snorting and stamping of the Minotaur. He drew his sword in preparation.

After a massive fight, the Minotaur was slain. Exhausted, Theseus followed the twine back to the entrance. Ariadne unlocked the doors and they rushed out to escape on the waiting ship.

But Theseus did not keep his promise to Ariadne—he left without her. Furious, Ariadne called to the gods for revenge, and Dionysus granted her wish. He made Theseus forget to hoist the white sail.

Aegeus was watching the sea for Theseus's return. At last, he saw a ship! But wait … was that a black sail? "My son is dead," groaned Aegeus. Unable to bear his grief, he jumped into the sea and drowned.

QUESTS AND ADVENTURES

Much of what we know about Greek mythology comes from the work of the famous poet Homer. He wrote two epic poems called the *Iliad* and the *Odyssey*. The ancient Greeks placed much value on his works, and some could recite them by heart. They were seen as important pieces of literature, but also as a guide to how to live a moral life.

THE ILIAD

The quests and adventures of Hector and Achilles are told in the *Iliad*, which is set during the Trojan War. This was a war between the Greeks and a place called Troy. The war continued for 10 years, and the gods took sides.

Achilles was the son of the mortal Peleus and the sea nymph Thetis. Achilles was a brave warrior of the Greek army. On the other side was Hector, son of the Trojan king Priam. He was the chief warrior of the Trojan army.

Achilles had an argument with another warrior, Agamemnon, and withdrew from the fighting. Hector took advantage of this and forced the Greeks back to their ships. Achilles's closest friend, Patroclus, came to help the Greeks but was killed by Hector. Achilles returned to avenge his friend's death and killed Hector.

Achilles showed no mercy and killed Hector.

WHO'S WHO?

We don't know much about Homer. He was thought to have lived during the 8th century BCE among the Greeks settled on the coast of modern Turkey. The ancient Greeks thought of Homer as a poor, blind minstrel.

Did you know?

Have you heard of an "Achilles' heel?" One story says that Thetis dipped Achilles into the waters of the River Styx to make him immortal. However, she was holding him by the part of the heel we now call our Achilles' heel, so this part didn't enter the water. This was the only place that Achilles was vulnerable.

Odysseus used his cunning to escape from Polyphemus's cave.

THE ODYSSEY

The *Odyssey* is shorter than the *Iliad* and describes the return of Odysseus from Troy. Odysseus's journey home is quite an adventure—he encounters the one-eyed giant Polyphemus, whom he blinds, and the cannibal giants who destroy all but one of his ships. In Thrinacia, Odysseus and his crew were warned not to kill the cattle of the sun god Helios. But they did, so as punishment Zeus destroyed their ship and crew with a thunderbolt. Now alone, Odysseus was washed up on the island of Ogygia. Here he met the goddess Calypso, who wanted to marry him. He refused because he already had a wife, but she kept him there for seven years. Eventually Zeus ordered his release.

WHO'S WHO?

Apollonius of Rhodes (3rd century BCE) wrote the epic poem *Argonautica*. The poem was in a similar style to Homer's epic poems and told the story of Jason and the Argonauts.

OTHER GREEK QUESTS

Two other great Greek heroes, Jason and Heracles, are famous for their quests. Jason is on a quest to fetch the Golden Fleece, which is thought to be an impossible task. His crew of 50 heroes traveled on the ship *Argo*, so were known as the Argonauts.

One of the Argonauts was Heracles. Famous for his great strength and courage, Heracles is known for having to complete 12 labors set as a punishment. These labors included killing a lion with his bare hands, killing a nine-headed dragon, and capturing flesh-eating horses.

WHO'S WHO?

Chiron was a wise centaur (half man, half horse) who gave advice to many Greek heroes, as well as some of the lesser gods. But he was accidentally killed by Heracles with a poisoned arrow.

Odysseus's Return Home

Deep down in the Underworld, Odysseus leaned in closely as the old soothsayer, Tiresias, told his future.

"You will return alone to your home in Ithaca," wheezed the old man. "You will find people fighting over your belongings."

"What about my wife? Is she still alive?" Odysseus begged Tiresias for more details, but the old soothsayer just walked away.

"I must get back home." Odysseus prayed to the gods. "Athena, will you still help me?"

Athena's voice came to him. "You must go home, but in disguise," she said. "There are many challenges to come, but I will help you."

It took a long time, but eventually Odysseus glimpsed the first sight of his home.

Disguised as an old beggar man, he approached the house and was greeted by his old swineherd, Eumaeus, who was kind to him but didn't recognize him.

Later, when he entered his house, Odysseus was shocked to see his wife, Penelope, surrounded by suitors. She was busy weaving as they argued together.

He heard her tell them, "Gentlemen, if you don't leave me to finish this weaving, I'll never decide who I am going to marry." Odysseus hid his sadness, realizing that Penelope thought he was dead.

Once the suitors had left, Penelope turned to chat with the strange old beggar man as she unpicked the day's weaving. She felt sorry for him and invited him to stay for dinner.

As Penelope prepared dinner, Odysseus was surprised to see the suitors return. Over dinner, Penelope told them all that she would marry the man who could string her husband's bow. The next morning, all the suitors tried and failed.

"Let me have a go," said the beggar man.

"You? Don't make me laugh!" said one of the suitors. But to their amazement, Odysseus easily strung the heavy bow. With a joyous cry, Penelope recognized her husband, home at last.

DEATH AND THE AFTERLIFE

The ancient Greeks believed in life after death. They believed that their souls went to the Underworld, which was an underground kingdom ruled by Hades. Sometimes this world was called Hades, too.

WHO'S WHO?

Charon was the person who would take souls across the River Styx to the Underworld. His payment would be one or two copper coins that the person's relatives would put in the dead person's mouth. If the soul had no money to make payment, then he would be left to wander on the bank.

THE ROUTE TO THE UNDERWORLD

The Greeks believed their souls would be guided by the god Hermes down to the River Styx. Here the soul was taken across the river by Charon, the ferryman. The entrance to the Underworld was guarded by Cerberus, a fierce three-headed dog. He let only the dead in and made sure no one left. A few people, such as Odysseus, were able to trick him.

PASSING JUDGMENT

When a soul first arrived in the Underworld, they would go before a panel of judges: Minos, Rhadamanthys, and Aeacus. These judges would pass sentence. Depending on how the person had behaved in life, he would be sent to one of three places. Ordinary people went to Asphodel Fields. This was a boring place where nothing much happened. The Elysian Fields was for the very good. And Tartarus was a place of punishment for evil people.

MYTH LINKS

The ancient Egyptians also believed that people would be judged in the afterlife. They believed that a person's soul would be weighed against "the feather of truth," and then the person would have to face the lord of the dead, Osiris. People hoped to live their next life in the Field of Reeds, which was an ideal version of Egypt.

VOYAGE TO THE UNDERWORLD

A few heroes made the voyage to the Underworld alive and returned to tell their tales. In Homer's *Odyssey* (see pages 30–33), the hero Odysseus visits the Underworld to learn about his destiny from Tiresias the soothsayer.

ODYSSEUS'S VOYAGE

Odysseus had been told that the winds would guide his ship to the Underworld. There he made offerings of milk, honey, wine, and water before entering. While he waited to speak to Tiresias, he met with one of his former companions, Elpenor. Odysseus promised to give him a proper burial so that his spirit could be at rest.

■ Tiresias is shown sitting, holding a knife, with Odysseus standing next to him.

After Tiresias offered advice as to how to return home safely, Odysseus met with several other spirits. He spoke to his mother, Anticlea, and to Agamemnon, Achilles, and other heroes. He also saw several people, such as Tantalus, being punished for things they had done during their lives.

ORPHEUS AND EURYDICE

Orpheus was the son of Apollo and was married to Eurydice. He was devastated when Eurydice died from a snake bite. He made the dangerous journey to the Underworld to persuade Hades to let him bring his wife back. Hades had just one condition—Orpheus was not to look at her until they were back in the land of the living. Orpheus could not resist taking a glimpse at her, though. But when he did, Eurydice was taken back to the Underworld by Hades.

MYTH LINKS

In Japan, there is a myth about the god Izanagi, who travels to the Land of the Dead to find his wife. But, like Persephone (see pages 38–39), she had already eaten the fruit of the dead and could not return.

Did you know?

The ancient Greeks thought many caves were entrances to the Underworld.

Persephone, Queen of the Underworld

As Persephone bent to pick the spring flowers, she heard a thunderous noise. Looking up in alarm, she saw the golden chariot of Hades appearing from beneath the earth.

"Father! Help me!" Persephone screamed to Zeus as Hades dragged her into his chariot. But it was no use—Zeus had allowed this. He had promised his daughter to Hades. Persephone was on her way down to the Underworld to become queen.

Persephone's mother, the goddess Demeter, knew nothing about the arrangement.

"Oh my sweet child! How could they do this to you?" Demeter sobbed. In despair, she neglected her role as goddess of plants and harvests to search for her daughter. Without her help, the earth became barren, everything died, and harvests failed.

People were dying, so the gods finally agreed that something needed to be done. Zeus sent Hermes to fetch Persephone back. But Hades had made Persephone eat a pomegranate, food of the Underworld.

"You can't come back," Zeus said sadly. "You've eaten food of the dead. It isn't allowed."

"But please father," begged Persephone. "Can't you do anything to help?"

Demeter added her own pleas. "Zeus, you've got to let her come back. I need her. Please—do this one thing for me."

Zeus thought for a bit. A plan was forming. "I can't let you come back forever. You ate that pomegranate, so you must spend part of the year with Hades. But for the rest of the year, you can be with your mother."

So for four months of the year, Persephone returns to her husband. Demeter is sad, the seasons turn to winter and nothing grows. But when it is time for Persephone to return to Earth, plants start to grow and flourish in the warm spring sunshine.

MYTHOLOGY
ALL AROUND US

While most of us probably can't recite Homer's poems, the myths of ancient Greece are still an influence on our culture today. Ancient Greek poets, such as Homer and Hesiod, have even influenced great writers such as Shakespeare.

Some Shakespeare plays, such as *Trolius and Cressida*, are based on Greek myth.

WHO'S WHO?

The ancient Greek philosopher Plato (5th–4th centuries BCE) was critical of the fictional (made-up) elements of myths, but many ancient Greeks believed the stories to be true.

What do you think of ancient Greek stories being turned into comic books?

INSPIRING PEOPLE

Characters from Greek mythology have inspired many artists and authors. If you are familiar with the Percy Jackson books and films, you'll know about the half boy, half god Percy, who is all hero. You may even recognize some of the character names, such as Poseidon, Ares, and Zeus. Publisher Marvel has adapted Homer's *Iliad* into comic book form and his *Odyssey* into a graphic novel.

Game-makers have adapted Greek and other mythologies of ancient history to create video games. There are games such as *Kid Icarus: Of Myths and Monsters*, *Age of Empires: Mythologies*, and a variety of games based on the adventures of heroes such as Heracles (or Hercules). Even SpongeBob SquarePants has gotten in on the action with the video game *SpongeBob & the Clash of Triton*!

MYTH LINKS

Today, names from Greek myths are used on products and businesses. Look out for travel agencies named "Atlas" or "Odyssey," courier services named "Pegasus," or perhaps even cement companies called "Medusa!"

And of course, who could forget the Olympic Games? They are the modern version of those games originally held to honor the supreme leader, Zeus.

CHARACTERS, CREATURES, AND PLACES

Look at the words in brackets to find out how to say these Greek names.

CHARACTERS

Achilles (a-kill-eez) hero of the *Iliad*; son of mortal Peleus and Thetis, the sea nymph

Aphrodite (aff-ro-die-tee) goddess of love and beauty

Apollo (a-poll-o) god of the sun and the arts; brother of Artemis and son of Zeus and Leto

Apollonius of Rhodes (a-poll-o-ni-us) author of *Argonautica*, the epic poem about Jason and the Argonauts

Ares (are-eez) god of war

Ariadne (a-ree-add-nee) daughter of King Minos who fell in love with Theseus

Artemis (are-tem-iss) goddess of hunting and light; sister of Apollo and daughter of Zeus and Leto

Athena (a-thee-na) goddess of war, wisdom, and arts and crafts; daughter of Zeus

Atlas (at-lass) one of the Titans; he was punished for fighting against Zeus by being made to support the heavens on his shoulders

Bellerophon (beel-air-oh-fon) hero who killed Chimera

Charon (ka-ron) the ferryman who takes dead souls across the River Styx to the Underworld

Cronus (kron-uss) king of the Titans; child of Gaia and Uranus. He was married to Rhea and was father to Zeus.

Demeter (de-meet-a) goddess of the earth, farming, and harvest; sister of Zeus; mother of Persephone

Dionysus (die-on-eye-sus) god of wine. He was the son of Zeus and a mortal called Semele.

Gaia (gay-a) a creator force that came out of the dark nothingness to create the world; also called Mother Earth

Hades (hay-deez) god of the Underworld; brother of Zeus and son of Cronus and Rhea; also called Pluto. He was the husband of Persephone. The Underworld is sometimes called Hades.

Hebe (hee-bee) goddess of youth

Hector (heck-tor) hero of the *Iliad*, son of Trojan king Priam. He was the chief warrior of the Trojan army.

Hephaestus (heff-eest-uss) god of fire and volcanoes

Hera (here-a) goddess of marriage and wife of Zeus; daughter of Cronus and Rhea

Heracles (here-a-kleez) hero; son of Zeus and mortal Alcmene; famous for his 12 labors

Hermes (her-meez) messenger of the gods; son of Zeus and Maia. He led the dead down to the Underworld.

Hestia (hess-tee-a) goddess of the hearth; daughter of Cronus and Rhea; sister of Zeus

Homer (home-er) ancient Greek poet who lived in about the 8th century BCE, he is thought to be the author of the *Iliad* and the *Odyssey*

Jason (jace-on) hero on a quest to fetch the Golden fleece with his crew of heroes on the ship *Argo*

Leto (lee-toe) a female Titan

Maia (my-a) a Titan; daughter of Atlas and mother to Hermes

Odysseus (oh-dee-see-us) hero of the *Odyssey*

Orpheus (or-fee-us) son of Apollo who voyages to the Underworld to get back his wife, Eurydice

Perseus (per-see-us) son of Zeus and Danae who killed Medusa the Gorgon

Plato (play-toe) ancient Greek philosopher

Poseidon (poss-eye-don) god of the sea, water, earthquakes, and horses; brother of Zeus and son of Cronus and Rhea. He is often shown holding a trident.

Rhea (ree-a) one of the Titans, married to Cronus. She sent her sixth child, Zeus, to Crete to stop Cronus from swallowing him.

Theseus (thee-see-us) hero who killed the Minotaur

Titans (tie-tans) offspring of Gaia and Uranus, they were strong giants who ruled Earth before the Olympian gods and goddesses took over

Zeus (zyoos) supreme leader of the Olympian gods and goddesses. He was the son of Cronus and Rhea. He was the god of sky, wind, clouds, rain, and thunder. He is often shown holding lightning bolts.

CREATURES

Cerberus (sir-ber-us) fierce, three-headed dog who guards the Underworld

Chimera (kim-ear-a) monster with the head of a lion, body of a goat, and rear of a serpent

Chiron (kheir-on) wise centaur killed accidentally by Heracles

Cyclopes (sye-klops) the first offspring of Gaia and Uranus, they were one-eyed giants

Medusa (med-yoo-sa) monster with snakes for hair who turned anyone who looked at her into stone

Minotaur (my-no-tore) half-bull, half-man creature

Pegasus (peg-a-suss) winged horse owned by Athena that sprang from the blood of Medusa the Gorgon

Polyphemus (pol-ee-fee-muss) one-eyed cyclops who trapped Odysseus in a cave

Typhon (tie-fon) monster with 100 serpent heads. Offspring of Gaia.

PLACES

Delphi (dell-fee) place where the Temple of Apollo was built

Knossos (nos-soss) place in Crete where it is thought King Minos had his palace and where the Minotaur might have lived

Mount Olympus (o-lim-puss) mountain in Greece where the gods and goddesses were thought to live

Parthenon (par-thee-non) temple in Athens built to honor Athena

River Styx (stiks) river that needs to be crossed to get to the Underworld

Sounion (su-nee-un) place where the Temple of Poseidon was built

Troy (t-roy) ancient city in what is now Turkey

GLOSSARY

altar table or flat block used as a place to make offerings or sacrifices to the gods

archaeologist person who studies the past by looking at human-made objects and remains

banish send away from a place as punishment

cannibal person who eats other human beings

chariot two-wheeled vehicle drawn by horses

city-state large community with an independent government

civilization society and culture of a particular area

epic long poem

ethylene gas gas found in natural gas, coal gas, and crude oil, and also given off by ripening fruit

immortal live forever; describes a being who cannot be killed

medicine man person thought to have magical healing powers, like a shaman

minstrel musician who sang or recited heroic poetry to music

mortal human being that will not live forever

omen event that might be a sign of good or evil

oracle message from the gods and deliverer of that message

rebellion fighting against the current ruler to try to take over as leader

sacrifice act of killing an animal or person as an offering to a god or goddess

sea nymph beautiful demigoddess (a lower rank of goddess)

shaman person thought to have contact with the world of good or evil spirits

soothsayer person who is thought to be able to tell the future

swaddling clothes cloth used to wrap a newborn baby in

Tartarus part of the Underworld where really evil people are punished

temple place of worship or home for a god or goddess

trance changed state of awareness of a person's environment

Trojan War war between the Greeks and the Trojans that lasted for 10 years, which is written about in Homer's the *Iliad*

Underworld place under earth where the dead went

FIND OUT MORE

BOOKS

DK Publishing. *Children's Book of Mythical Beasts and Magical Monsters*. New York: DK Children, 2011.

Homer. *The Odyssey*. Translated by E. V. Rieu. New York: Penguin, 2003.

Hunt, Jilly. *Greece*. Chicago: Heinemann Library, 2012.

Milbourne, Anna. *Usborne Book of Greek Myths*. Eveleth, Minn.: Usborne Books, 2010.

Napoli, Donna Jo. *Treasury of Greek Mythology*. Des Moines, Iowa: National Geographic Children's Books, 2011.

Turnbull, Ann. *Greek Myths*. Somerville, Mass.: Candlewick, 2010.

WEB SITES

www.ancientgreece.co.uk
The British Museum's web site has lots of information about ancient Greece, as well as challenges and games.

www.bbc.co.uk/history/ancient/greeks
Find out more about the ancient Greeks on BBC's Primary History site.

edweb.sdsu.edu/people/bdodge/scaffold/gg/greek_myth.html
This site is a good reference for information about ancient Greek mythology and compares Greek and Roman mythology.

www.museumnetworkuk.org/myths
Explore this site to find out more about Greek myths.

www.pantheon.org
Encyclopedia Mythica is an online encyclopedia of mythology, folklore, and religion.

PLACES TO VISIT

Use the Internet to research more places to visit where you can learn about ancient Greek myths and culture.

The Metropolitan Museum of Art
New York, New York
www.metmuseum.org
The Met has a gallery dedicated to ancient Greek and Roman art.

Ashmolean Museum
Oxford, England
www.ashmolean.org
The Ashmolean has one of the oldest and largest collections of ancient Greek and Roman sculpture.

The British Museum
London, England
www.britishmuseum.org
The British Museum has a gallery dedicated to Greek and Roman life.

National Archaeological Museum of Athens
Athens, Greece
www.namuseum.gr/wellcome-en.html
This museum is entirely devoted to ancient Greek art.

FURTHER RESEARCH

Perhaps you are interested in finding out more about how the Greek myths spread into other cultures? For instance, the ancient Romans were particularly influenced by Greek mythology. Or perhaps you want to know more about how the ancient Greeks lived or the history of the Olympic Games? You could use your local library and the Internet to find out more.

INDEX